Rose Petals
of
Serenity 2

By Serenity Poetry

serenitypoetry@gmail.com

Formatting, Cover Art, and Graphics by True Beginnings Publishing.
Author picture Photography by Geoffrey Paugam.
All Illustrations, Cover Art, and Text are Copyright Protected by:
My Original Works. Reference #73449.

To Contact the Publisher, please email at:
true_beginnings_publishing@yahoo.com

Ordering Information:
To order additional copies of this book, visit Amazon or please visit:
https://www.createspace.com/4965660

ISBN-10: 0692281215
ISBN-13: 978-0692281215

Rose Petals of Serenity
© Serenity Poetry
First Printing, 2014

Table of Contents

Midnight Write....The Poetry in ME

This poetry, the poetry in me has always been there. It's a love/hate relationship. At least that's how it started. She always loved me, and I loved her as long as her message was happy and cheery. As long as it made me smile and bubbly inside. When she took a turn to the dark side and made me face what hides in the dark, I hated her. I avoided her. Years at a time I pretended she didn't exist within me. I cheated at times because there were too many writers who embraced her. So I indulged in the happiness they provided me.

Poetry, she always loved me. She knew I'd be back. I always returned because she really is beauty. I learned to love her fully. And embrace her and accept her. She is in ME. I learned that my light is much too bright to be dulled by anything in the dark, and my poetry will shine all the days of my life.

My poetry.... is beauty... my poetry..... is ME.

Dedication

This book is dedicated in loving memory of my mother, Bonnie Lynn Ward. I love you, always.

To my children, Darien, James and Lynn. You are my world, and I will continue to work to make you all proud of me. I love you with all that I am.

Butterflies

He asked what I wanted.
I replied, "The man to share my life with,
The man who can give me butterflies every time I see him."
With that statement, he was amused;
Asking about butterflies, years into a relationship?
My reply, "Of course, have you ever heard a golden couple talk
about their love? They smile and talk about butterflies."
THAT'S what I want!
Bypassing insignificant arguments for the simple fact
They're insignificant!
The man who I put first because I know
He puts me first.
That was just the beginning.
I smiled as I expressed my desires,
And he listened with a look of awe on his face,
Nodding in agreement and occasionally finishing my thoughts.
I want a man whose jagged edges of his imperfections fit perfectly
with my own, creating a beautiful jigsaw puzzle of our lives
becoming one.
And as I thought more of what I wanted,
I realized more that I actually deserved it.
He cooked for me and served me.
I could certainly get used to that.

We were at our own interview.
What do we want
And what do we do
When we find "The One."

If I Must

I will not be stopped;
My purpose in life will be fulfilled.
My destiny, reached;
All obstacles set to deter me
Are invisible.
As I strive to be my own best,
Better than I was, yesterday,
Constantly searching for improvements, today,
So that I may Excel tomorrow,
Knowing that disappointments
Are inevitable.
I'm prepared
As I sit in reflection,
Ready to stand for my beliefs
And lay down my life for the truth.
I'll be a warrior for my own honor
If I must.

No Words

Not often am I left without words.
I've found myself there,
Wishing to have answers
To questions that haven't been asked yet.
Knowing that "It will get better" doesn't quite suffice
For the matter at hand,
With an understanding that time really does heal all wounds.
But what if even I am not so sure
As I see the wounds as they are formed,
Imagining what scars will be left behind,
Not sure how to even nurse them.
And so, I pray.
I pray for the right words to say
To comfort.
If there are no words,
I pray for the strength and ability
To just be.
I pray to just be the voice of reason,
A peaceful spirit,
A friend.
When I'm at a loss of words,
I pray my presence will be enough
In a time of healing.

My Jesus

I saw the Passion of Christ
For the very first time
On Good Friday.
I nearly cried.
Everyone knows about His life and death.
Not everyone believes.
As for me,
I believe,
And I know
That he lives.
For all my years on this planet,
I never imagined just what was written.
The Passion of Christ brought his crucifixion to life.
It brought the death of Jesus to LIFE.
To imagine THAT sacrifice,
"Forgive them Father."
To think that he died for me,
"They know not what they do."

He died so I could live.
Thank you feels inadequate,
So I pray that each day
Finds me a better woman than the previous,
And I give thanks for each day I open my eyes.
I live the best life I can through HIM,
And I thank GOD for the sacrifice of HIS Son for my life.

Understanding

I hate
When my words
Betray me.
All I have are my words.
They get twisted and mingled,
Causing these
Misunderstandings,
And I hate
When what's in my head
And what is said
Or heard
Don't quite match up.
It weighs heavy on my mind
When we aren't on the same page
Of the same book.
I need for you to understand,
And I need for you to follow
My thoughts.
These Misunderstandings
Are really pissing me off.
I feel they are like a wedge between us;
Each one increasing the gap between us.

Can we break this down?
Get the words to line up?
We need understanding,
And it starts with
US.

I Wonder

I wonder if they know.
Is it possible for them to know
That I thrive on their energy?
I write for them as much as I write for me.
I write to share my story,
Yet to let them know
That I know
What they go through.
And I wonder if they know
How I love to see their comments
And read how they feel
After sharing my own feelings.
And the support;
What can I possibly say about the undying support?
I love it, and I love them.
Each person who shows support
Means so much to me.
I wonder if they know
How I love the positivity I see.
I will always Thank them
And appreciate them
For allowing me to share
My life.

Seaside Evening

Have you ever seen the reflection of the moon on the ocean in the
late evening?
After the sunbathers have long since gone
And children splashing in the water is just a mere memory.
Taking in a picnic under the stars
With the tastiest of all fruits, and maybe a bottle of champagne.
The music is none other than waves crashing on the shore
As you lie back and stare at each constellation and dream,
Wishing on a falling star.
Have you ever smelled the fresh air by the seashore?
It soothes your mind, body and soul with each breath you take.
Walking barefoot on the sand,
Dipping your toes in the water,
Memories of a time of innocence,
Yet a constant reminder of new beginnings
As the waves wash away fresh footprints in the sand.
When was the last time you took in a seaside evening?
I think you're over due.

*Tender moments are
to be treasured.*

*Sadly, they end far
too soon.*

~Serenity~

Time Stood Still

I have experienced time standing still.
It was that day
He and I talked and allowed our conversation to silence itself.
We shared a tender moment,
I was in his embrace,
And he was in mine.
The chatter of the world around us
Distanced itself from us.
In that moment, only he and I existed.
As he closed his eyes and rested his head on my bosom,
I slowly rested my chin atop his head,
Not sure what to do
Or even if I needed to do anything.
I too closed my eyes and just...... was.
I was comfortable in my state of mind,
To just let go of every conscience thought.
I let go of my worries and doubts,
I let go of what society taught me,
And I just enjoyed him.
I enjoyed the tender moment,
I enjoyed his embrace,
And I recited my poetry,
Whispering in his ear.

He was all that I saw,
And his voice was the only voice I heard,
And I felt him, not his touch.
I felt his soul,
And it was beautiful.
I listened to every word he never spoke,
I saw the secrets he never shared.
When he opened his eyes,
And I looked in,
Time stood still.

Lost

I needed to lose myself;
To find these words
In the midst of being lost;
The realization that my subconscious
Supercedes my conscious
In the imagination department
Is no longer denied.
And so, I will happily accept defeat
In the name of art;
Holding the white flag up
In exchange for the opportunity
To once again fall in love with my own creation.
I'll call that heaven.
I can't imagine a better place to find myself submerged,
Drowning in my own creativity,
Holding my breath as I search
For that perfect time to again exhale,
Being lost in my own words,
Allowing them to show me the way.
I'll take that any day.

I haven't written.
I tried to control it,
And the writing showed me
Who was boss.
Poetry whispered in my ear,
"Let go! Trust me, I got this."
I obediently listened,
And I wrote.

7

7

I had a dream about seven.
It came to me and refuses to leave.
I was told all evil ends at seven,
And the countdown continues.
7

And on the seventh day, he rested.
A broken mirror brings 7 years bad luck.
Even debt is erased after 7 years,
And my seven is so close.
7

Reviewing my own experiences,
Adding up each roadblock,
Counting the attacks on my character,
Crossing off each 7 that's reached.
7

In my quest to find an answer,
Spirituality was at the base,
Allowing self to be lost,
And patiently awaiting for 7 to find me.

7
Came to me in a dream.
I search for truth,
And seven remains with me
Until the final seven is reached.

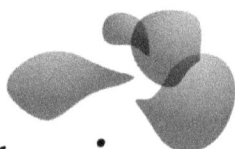

*Every day isn't going
to be great.
Those not-so-great days
help us appreciate.
Smile knowing that
it will get better.*

~Serenity~

Rain

The only time I like the rain
Is when I want it to hide my tears;
The tears that only come
When I can no longer handle the pain,
And the sounds of the rain drops
Drown out everything else.
I wait for the rain to stop
With hopes that it also
Leaves a clean slate.

The only time I like the rain
Is when life gets chaotic,
And the world is forced to slow down.
Proceed with caution,
Watch for standing water,
Being forced to reflect,
And tend to what I easily neglect.

And as the rain falls,
And the lightning and Thunder calls,
I watch and listen,
Playing catch up with myself,
Because I've allowed my thoughts to be run wild.

The only time I like the rain
Is when it stops;
Looking for the rainbow,
Because the rain never lasts for too long,
A constant reminder that it gets better.
The storms must come,
The rains must come,
And it always gets better.

Good Conversation

Good conversation,
Give me your good conversation,
And I'll give you the same in return.
It's your intellect that I desire
And your sense of humor.
Keep my mind occupied for hours.
Make me fall in love with your voice
As I take in each syllable of each word,
Breaking down the verbs,
Nouns and pronouns to just letters;
Reassembling them to form my own words;
The pregnant silence as you do the same in return.
Let me get lost in your stories
While our imaginations play childhood games of yesterday.

Tag.
You're it.
Pick up where I left off
With closed eyes, I'll follow.
Tease me with your wordplay;
I can listen to that all day.
Each analogy and metaphor
Has me begging you for more.
Give me your good conversation.

Her Innocence

Her innocence reminds me of my childhood,
In a time where my own mommy knew all the answers.
As we enjoy our own mommy/daughter time,
She asks me question after question.
I answer.
She sits, absorbing all that I tell her,
Randomly giving hugs,
Which in return draws kisses.
Her innocence reminds me of
Rolling down the hill in a race with my siblings,
Block parties ending the summer,
Modeling my new wardrobe every spring and fall,
Running in the water from the fire hydrant on a hot day,
Ice Cream from Mr.Softee.
I try to preserve her innocence.
She deserves to have such happy memories.
Let her remember me the way I remember my mommy.
When she asks me how to speak Spanish,
I answer,
And we talk until she has no more questions.
Her innocence reminds me,
And I need for her to remember.

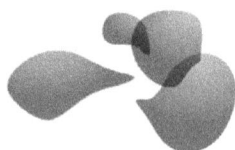

*You never miss what
is given from the heart.*

*The heart automatically
replenishes itself.*

~Serenity~

Love's Rehab

I learned at an early age that
I....... am........ a........ LOVER.
I love.
I love hard,
I love deep,
I love true.
I love when perhaps they have never known love,
And I leave myself exposed.
As a result of my being a lover,
I've found myself checking in again,
After promising myself that the last time was
The last time.
Determined to get it right next time,
Saving myself from myself,
Put my feelings in a jar on the shelf,
Collect my thoughts,
Wait for the time I can receive the mutual feelings that are sought.
Give and give and give
Is the only way I know how to live.
I am addicted to love,
There is no 12 step program,
And if there's a cure, I certainly don't want it.
This love thing.

I'll go to rehab, time and time again,
Until I get it right,
And this love thing
Is worth the countless visits to rehab,
Because when it's right…
Well, when it's right…
There will be no words.
Yet, my pen will never rest,
Because this love thing
That lives in me
Deserves to be immortalized.
Love deserves that.

Detached

I sat across from him,
Determined to keep my cool.
I spoke in a calm manner
With a slight smile on my lips.
After 1/2 dozen court appearances,
We had scored an appointment with a family counselor,
And I kept my cool.
He wasn't ready.
I'm emotional,
And I've been emotional,
Every
Single
Time.
Crying before the judge,
Emotional outbursts,
Screaming he's a liar.
Emotions don't mix well with court.
The mental preparations
Never left me prepared.
The emotional warfare
Had taken a toll.
Constant reminders to stay calm
Were forgotten.

But that day
With the counselor,
I kept my cool.
He saw what had happened,
And my voice was heard
When I could speak my peace,
And keep cool.
I was finally heard.
He wasn't ready.
All he could say in his own emotional outburst,
"She's detached!"

I Fell In Love

I fell in love once.
Not to be mistaken with loving another;
I've loved other times,
And been loved in return a few times,
But being in love?
I was there once.
The best way to explain it;
We didn't need words,
We felt,
We laughed for hours at nothing in particular,
We just were.
I never could physically get close enough to him.
I needed to be one with him.
It was intense.
When I looked in his eyes,
I saw my own reflection.
The freedom to just be me,
And he,
Well he loved it,
Until he didn't,
Because it became intense.
That need to be one
Was more than he could handle.

He had never be in love either.
And that feeling.
That overwhelming desire
Of becoming one with another.
Was a feeling he couldn't accept.
We never will be one.
We are two
Living separate lives;
Just a memory to the other
Of when we fell in love.

Sleep Didn't Escape

Last night,
I didn't write.
The silence hushed,
And I slept.
My thoughts allowed me to rest;
There were no poems begging to be born.
Sleep didn't escape me,
There was no over sensitivity,
My mind was at ease,
And allowed the body to rest.
The tears I cry late in the wee hours
Didn't fall.
The Silent prayers for a change,
Those prayers of a single mother
Didn't slip through my lips.
Thoughts of what may come today,
Last night even they stayed away.
Baby girl cuddled next to me.
I watched her sleep.

I felt myself dozing off.
With a smile, I thought,
Tonight
I
Will
Sleep.
Sleep didn't escape me.

As I Am

His words echo down to my inner core,
"You deserve much more."
I had for a split second forgotten how to breathe.
I mean, he was that breath of fresh air;
The first and last thought of the day,
The reason I thought I would love again.
He was what I had not seen before in a man.
No, he wasn't supernatural,
But he had something about him,
And I knew that it wasn't to last,
But I had fooled myself
To think my feelings of doubt would pass.
And no,
This wasn't physical,
And for him it wasn't personal.
He saw me
As I am.
His job was simply
To help me see myself
As I am.

But the echo won't stop,
"You deserve much more."
And I wish I had just listened to myself
When the doubts surfaced.
Perhaps, it might have helped me save face.
"You deserve much more."
Yes, I deserve much more.
As I reviewed my own words of the past,
I read poem upon poem,
Over and over.
Some, I had forgotten about.
I am poetry,
Yet, I had forgotten some of ME.
The more I read,
The more I came to see,
He saw me as I am,
He saw the God in me.
It was only then that I could repeat,
"I deserve much more."

April Foolishness

I don't play pranks,
Especially not today.
Honestly,
Who will actually make an important announcement
On April 1?
Before I became a mother, I told friends, "I'm pregnant."
Being my quiet, shy self,
Yes ,THAT was surprising.
But I don't play pranks.
Perhaps, a small joke
That is totally unexpected
On an unexpected day.
So, there are no April Fools being told to my kids.
I felt a bit silly,
But her father told her,
And she became a class clown.
I won't lie,
When she said "April Foolishness,"
I laughed.
I thought to myself, "You got that right, baby girl."

Silent Prayers

I haven't eaten much,
And sleep has become a distant memory.
The twinkle is missing from my eyes,
And the smile seems out of place.
In the blink of an eye,
I lost myself.
With burdens heavier then I imagined,
And my conscience leading the way,
A cluttered mind, with random thoughts
Occupying far too much time,
Silent prayers lost in the wind,
Weakness of flesh leading to sin,
Wide awake,
Yet sleeping on my faith,
Repeating to myself
I am a child of GOD,
Remembering forgotten prayers.
My story is already written,
This life is my blessing,
Embracing my own choices,
Listening to the inner voices,
I'm destined for greatness.
Silent prayers lost in the wind.

I'm destined for greatness.
Let the wind carry my silent prayers
To the heavens, above.
The tests may push me to limits,
I will never lose my self-love.
Silent prayers
Carried by the wind
Are always answered.

Real Love Waits

I handed him my shattered heart,
Piece by piece,
In an effort
To find my peace,
And he held it, gently,
As though it were the most fragile crystal ever bestowed upon him,
Determined to nurse each fracture
And mend each crack;
Sure to reinforce with care, attention and love,
With a promise to forever protect it.
He nurtured my broken heart
With words of encouragement.
He brought life back
And showed how a man should love a woman.
He showed me
Love,
Patiently waiting
For the day the broken heart beat, again,
And patiently waiting
For it to skip a beat for him.
I had won his heart at first glance,
While all he asked from me was a chance;
A chance to show me that love…
Real love…
Will wait.

Forever.....

He said he would love me forever,
But forever didn't last as long as I thought it would be.
He is no longer with me.
I asked him will you still love me if I gain weight,
And will you still love me when my hair gets Grey?
(I was feeling Music Soulchild)
He said yes.
"WE" didn't last that long.
I was totally committed,
While he was afraid of commitment
With me.
The final remnants of him
Make their way out of my life,
But the memories,
They just don't stop;
A constant reminder
Of a love lost;
A reminder that forever really
Isn't
Forever.

A reminder that "WE"
Never were meant to be.
A reminder that, sometimes…
Sometimes, good things come to an end.
A reminder that forever
Doesn't exist
In love.

I Wanted To Write A Poem

I wanted to write a poem about him,
But the words wouldn't come to me.
I wanted to share how I felt,
But the words escaped me.
I sat,
And I thought,
And I felt,
And I sought.
Still .... No words.
Then, it dawned on me.
I could not write about him;
I didn't want him to be a memory.
I needed him to be with me,
And I just needed him.
I hope the words never come
For me to write about him.
We will be living our dreams,
Making memories.

I can't write about him.
He gets me
When I need to write.
It will be a handwritten letter to him,
And I'll whisper my secrets
In his ear,
And I'll show him how I need him near.
I'll say what I need to say
To him, daily.
We'll live our dreams,
Making them reality.
As for our memories,
One day
We'll look back on them,
But for now,
I'll let the words escape me,
For he's not a memory.

*Everything you
go through is
preparation for where
you are meant to be.*

~Serenity~

I Tried To Cry

I tried to cry.
I had already cried my eyes dry.
As the pain of loss started to dull,
Though it was dulling,
It was still there.
Still hurting,
Still
There.
And I tried to cry,
Because relief comes
After the tears.
I couldn't get back the years
That caused the ache
And heartbreak.
I always come with a warning,
Take heed to the warning,
Listen to my words,
I know me,
And I know that learning me
Isn't easy.
If your patience is thin,
Then keep your application.

My love is mine to give,
And when I do,
Stay positive,
Because I can't take another heartbreak.
My eyes
No longer allow me to cry,
And the pain,
It hurts.

I Am Poetry

The Passion

He told me it was my passion that first caught his attention;
Passion for life,
Passion for living,
Passion for the search to keep giving,
Giving of myself in my poetry.
He said he just wanted to have a drink with me
And drink in all of me.
Not me,
But my thoughts.
He wanted to get lost,
Feel my pains,
Share my triumphs.
He wanted to feel me.
He wanted to know me.
He was attracted to my passion.
I slowly revealed it to him,
What makes me smile.
He put the twinkle back in my eye,
And the pains of past love?
It started to fade.
I no longer wrote about the pain;
I found better days.

And I wrote.
I wrote what was on my mind
And in my heart.
The fire in me
And the desire in me,
Allowed my pen to bleed.
The passion…
It's the Passion that allows me to do this.
He was attracted to the Passion in me.
It's the Passion that allows my pen to bleed.

The Forgotten Art

It starts with a blank sheet of paper,
A pen,
And an avalanche of feelings.
It's a work of art.
Emotions turned into something tangible,
A handwritten letter,
A simple thought,
A simple thought sparking an urge
To create.
Spoken words
Can only be heard
Once,
But a written letter
Often expressing thoughts better;
Will be read and re-read,
Perhaps catching words left unsaid.
Instant gratification
Is not the motivation
Behind a handwritten letter.
Informally, formal,
Unmistakably personal,
Flaunting the personality of the writer.

It is said you can tell a great deal about someone by how they write.
The handwritten letter
Demands to be read.
Let the thoughts and ideas marinate, if you will.

I Want To

I want to
Experience you.
Let me close my eyes
As you tell me a story, or two.
Visualize every last syllable,
Smiling at the Highs,
Eyes welling with tears at the Lows,
As each moment of your day,
You expose
To me.
I'll feel the excitement in your voice
As the story picks up speed,
And my adrenaline will rush
Visualizing you smiling.
Inhale.
Exhale.
Your mannerisms excite me.
The way you pause mid-sentence
Fills me with anticipation.
Don't.
Stop.

Hanging on your words
As though they are my own breath.
Breathe life into me
As your story takes a turn.
Words becoming inaudible.
I.
Struggle.
Lack of oxygen.
Your tears fall from my eyes.
Why?
Because I feel you,
And the disappointments you've gone through.
Mouth to mouth resuscitation,
Breathe life into me.
Your words…
Your words save me.
Let me
Experience you.
Give me your words.
I'll close my eyes
And come to life.

Each day is 24
hours to do
something
AMAZING!

~Serenity~

Who I Was Made To Be

I was born to do this
Even before I knew what THIS was.
The tiniest Flicker of a flame,
The discouragements came,
But the feelings remained.
Dreams deferred,
Future on the list of "Unsure."
No more.
I thought my dreams were dead,
But he felt a pulse there
And gave them mouth to mouth resuscitation.
A bellows to a dying flame,
Helping to get them going as though they just took a vacation.
Being lost for too long,
Searching for the perfect song.
I'm not very good with metaphors;
I sit and pen my emotions raw.
In marching to the beat of a different drummer,
I found my voice.
I don't fit in the mold of a cookie cutter.
You either love me or hate me.
This is who I was made to be.

Makidada

You and I will never part,
Makidada.
As little girls,
We played Barbies late into the night,
Passed our bedtime
And all day on Sunday,
With plots filled with enough drama
To rival daytime soap operas.
These little perfect, plastic dolls
You and me, us have one heart,
Makidada,
The eldest daughters of Bonnie Lynn.
We grew closer,
Leaning on each other,
Helping, supporting and loving,
Both imitating our mother,
Hosting baby showers,
And being proud aunties
To perfect newborn babies.
Ain't no ocean, ain't no sea,
Makidada.

Now, adults with families of our own,
Living different lives,
But almost daily talks on the phone;
Closer now than we were as little girls
With pigtails and curls.
Keep my sister away from me…

I'm A Woman

I never claimed to be perfect.
I'm a woman.
I forget more than I will admit.
However, it doesn't mean I care any less.
With a memory like mine,
Lying is not an option.
I love wholeheartedly,
And I will give you my all,
But perfect I am not.
Karma is real to me,
So deceitful actions
Don't make much sense to me.
My desire is always to be better
Than I was, yesterday,
Which will never be as good
As I will be, tomorrow.
I never claimed to be perfect.
I have a forgiving spirit,
And I always strive to be the best
I can possibly be.
I've experienced more than any woman should,
But less than many have.

I wake each morning, not knowing
Just what's in store for me,
As though each day is an adventure in itself.
Looking at life through the eyes of an innocent child,
Because it's those childlike, innocent thoughts
That help me to see the good in all things,
And though I see the good in all things,
Even a child learns that though fire is magical,
It only takes one burn to learn that it's hot.
I never claimed to be perfect.
Maybe, perfectly flawed.
As I learned to embrace the imperfections,
I realized I'm perfectly the way I was made to be.
I'm a woman.
I've given up when I should have fought,
And fought when I should have given up.
I've loved when they didn't deserve it, been mistreated,
Lord knows I didn't deserve it.
Thought that I could change the world,
And I did, maybe not THE WORLD,
But the world FOR someone.
I never claimed to be perfect,
But Someone thinks I am.

Acknowledgements

Thank you to my sister, Jennell Lozin, so much for your love and support in simply living day to day. As we take the lessons of our childhood and realize the core of the words, "Your sister is your best friend." Seeing life from different views and appreciating the varieties it offers. I will love you, always, Makidada.

My brother, Thomas Ward Jr. For always being there, even with miles separating us. Your love and support has always shown through, no matter what we are experiencing.

To my sister, Jeanette Ward. I love you, Sis.

My aunts, Lisa Hooks, Denise Thompson, Faith Gibbs.... And uncles, Dennis Hooks, Keith Hooks and Darryl Hooks. I love you all so much. Our blood line runs long and thick. You each are constant in my life and a reminder of the lessons my own mother instilled in me about family.

Uncle Chris and Aunt Victoria Ward. Thank you for being my first lessons of following your dreams, no matter what everyone says. When you have passion and determination, expect manifestation.

Willy Lozin, Sheila Hooks, Ronald Gibbs, all of my cousins (far too many to name). I love you all dearly for your love and support! I have the absolute BEST family.

Jeff Farley, L. Michelle, Marion Rogers, Tina Aurrichio: I Thank you all for being there for me with your undying friendship and support. At some point, our conversations hit home, and you helped push me a little further in my craft. There are no words for that gratitude.

To everyone who simply finds peace within my words, I thank you. You are my inspiration.

Last but certainly not least, thank you to my father, Thomas Ward. Thank you for being a good father as I grew into the woman I am. Teaching me lessons throughout my life that will remain with me as I continue to share my story through poetry.

Serenity was born in the diverse and fast moving Queens, New York. During her childhood, however, she wound up moving around and eventually settling in South Florida. All these places only gave her a better view of the world and what it has to offer.

Serenity was always a fan of the arts and found herself taking dance, drawing, sketching and writing, as well. However, it was the passing of her grandmother that had Serenity writing her first original poem. Life experience after life experience gave her the fuel and inspiration to create "Answer True"- a piece that got attention from not only people in her circle, but other poets, as well. In November 2010, she took the stage for the first time at Verbal Calligraphy. There, she performed one of her most requested works to date, "Superwoman."

Serenity prides herself on making poetry that helps others through the adversity in their lives. Recently, she has begun work on two major projects "Serenity in a Sea of Chaos," an audio album, and a book "Rose Petals of Serenity" to reach more people, worldwide. Her influences range from Maya Angelou to Nikki Giovanni to Langston Hughes.